ANCIENT EGYPT

TOUGH TIMES to Be a Kid

Written by
Hermione Redshaw

BookLife PUBLISHING

©2023
BookLife Publishing Ltd.
King's Lynn, Norfolk
PE30 4LS, UK

All rights reserved.
Printed in Poland.

A catalogue record for this book is available from the British Library.

ISBN: 978-1-80155-849-5

Written by:
Hermione Redshaw

Edited by:
Robin Twiddy

Designed and illustrated by:
Amy Li

All facts, statistics, web addresses and URLs in this book were verified as valid and accurate at time of writing. No responsibility for any changes to external websites or references can be accepted by either the author or publisher.

CONTENTS

Page 4	Being a Kid
Page 6	Ancient Egypt
Page 8	Surviving the Time
Page 10	Family is Forever
Page 12	Walls as Thin as Paper
Page 14	Fishy Business
Page 16	Eaten by the Gods
Page 18	Horrible Hairstyles
Page 20	Splinters and Senet
Page 22	Writing in Pictures
Page 26	Grown Up at What Age?
Page 30	That's Tough!
Page 31	Glossary
Page 32	Index

Words that look like this are explained in the glossary on page 31.

Being a KID

It's tough being a kid. A bad haircut can ruin your week. Teachers keep making schoolwork harder. Your parents always go on about how good it is to share things.

Imagine you live in a time when your textbooks are written in strange pictures, you share your bedroom with your entire family and your hair has to be shaved on one side throughout your childhood. Now, you have just imagined what it was like to live in ancient Egypt.

If you think being a kid is tough today, you may want to prepare yourself. What you are about to read might make you think again. Ancient Egypt really was a tough time to be a kid.

ANCIENT EGYPT

So, get ready and let's travel back in time. Take a look for yourself at what life was really like for a child in ancient Egypt.

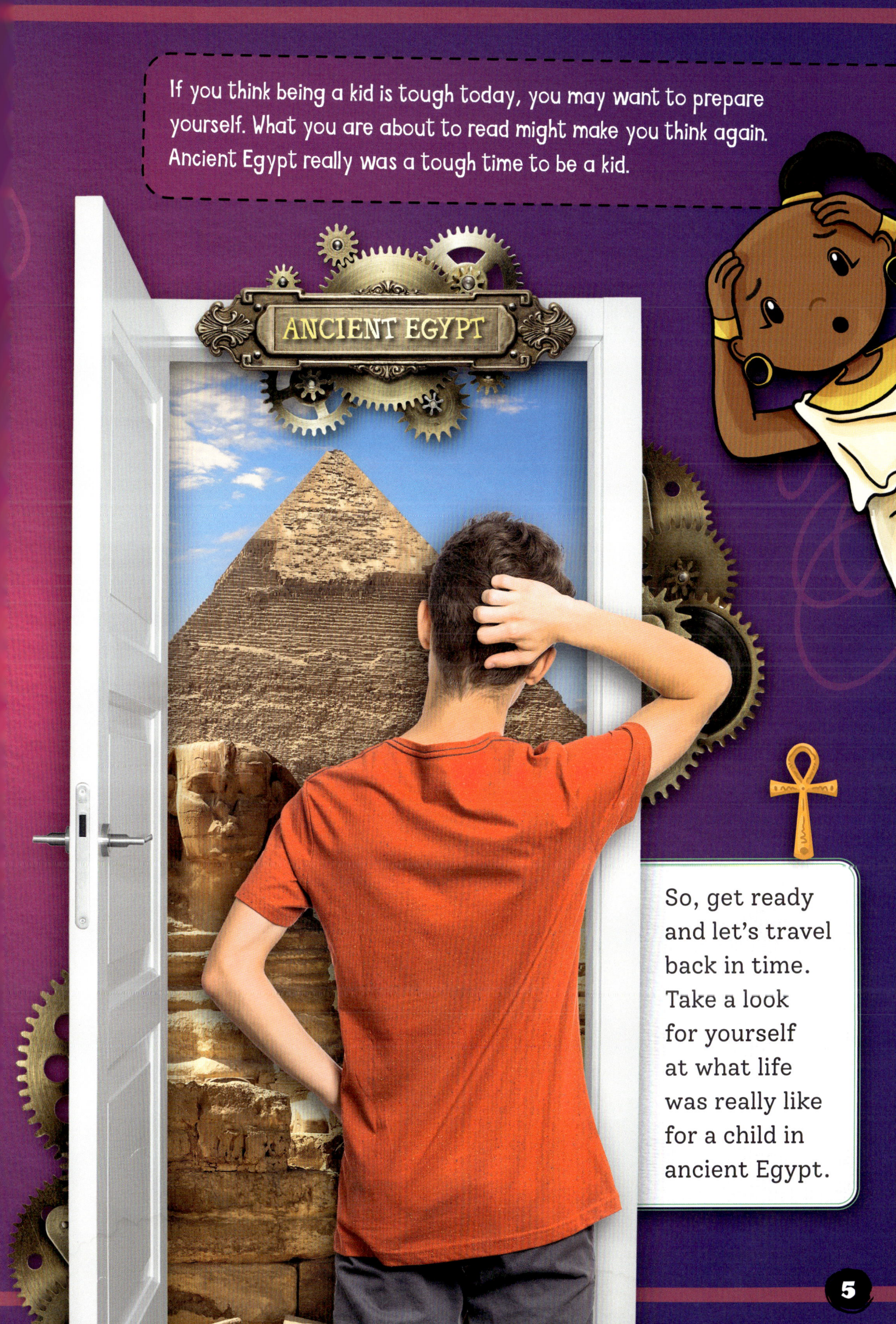

Ancient EGYPT

Ancient Egypt began around 5,000 years ago in the valley of the Nile River. From around 3100 BC to 30 BC, the ancient Egyptians built amazing things such as the pyramids, which can still be seen in Egypt today.

My breath is fresh thanks to the ancient Egyptians!

The Egyptians helped to create one of the first written languages. They even made paper to write it on. It is also thanks to the ancient Egyptians that we have toothpaste to keep our teeth clean.

"I'd much rather be doing a jigsaw right now!"

The impressive things that the ancient Egyptians gave us might surprise you with how different they were back then. Paper didn't just come in books or sheets like we have today. It had to be <u>woven</u> from thin pieces of a plant called papyrus.

"This toothpaste is a little sharp!"

You might think twice about putting ancient Egyptian toothpaste in your mouth. First, you had to gather the things that went into it and mash them up into a paste yourself. The <u>ingredients</u> included flowers, mint leaves and rock salt! They didn't stop there, though. Some people added burnt eggshells to the mix!

SURVIVING the Time

Surviving your childhood might seem easy to you. Your parents do most of the work, giving you food, a warm home and internet. Doctors can always take a look at you if you're feeling ill. However, surviving in ancient Egypt was a whole different game!

It sounds like the Egyptians were playing life on hard mode!

As many as half of ancient Egypt's children might not have lived past their first birthday, let alone survive all the way to adulthood. Many <u>diseases</u> that could be cured today were deadly in ancient Egypt.

I'm so lucky to have lived this long!

Some of the earliest written information about <u>medicine</u> came from ancient Egypt. That doesn't mean their medicine was any good, though. For most, healing the sick was done by praying. For some, doctors had <u>natural</u> medicines, which might have been made from plants or herbs.

There were other things to watch out for than doctors. Ancient Egypt was home to lots of scorpions and snakes. Don't think you'll come away with just a plaster over a scratch after a clash with one of those!

HEY! Watch where you're walking!

FAMILY is Forever

Families get on our nerves sometimes, but we love them anyway... most of the time. However, living under one roof can feel crowded at times. It's even worse when you've got a large family, and families in ancient Egypt were large!

The sofa isn't big enough for her too!

Family really is forever. There's no escaping it!

Even after a child grew up and got married, that didn't always mean they would move out. You could be living with all of your brothers, sisters, aunts, uncles and cousins for the rest of your life! That's not even including their husbands, wives and children of their own!

Ancient Egyptian children were sometimes called 'the staff of their father's old age'. That means you would have to help out your father, especially as he got older. Yes, even once you have left home, expect to pop back to help whenever Dad calls.

Son, help your granddad.

Not fair!

Son, I need your help.

Mothers were very important to the ancient Egyptians. They had their own Mother's Day all those thousands of years ago. There was also a celebration called mother's feast. Mothers and fathers often shared the role of looking after the house.

Respect Mum. She's the boss!

WALLS as Thin as Paper

Houses in ancient Egypt were made from things such as mud bricks. They even used papyrus at one time. Hold on, isn't papyrus the stuff that makes paper? There were no forests in ancient Egypt, meaning wood was hard to find. Let's hope those papyrus reeds are strong enough to keep your muddy home standing!

This really is a full house!

Most houses didn't have lots of rooms. They often had around three. This does not mean three bedrooms, though. Two of those would be your kitchen and living room. Remember all those family members that were mentioned earlier? Yes, all of them could be sharing one bedroom together!

Perhaps you're still thinking positively about your ancient Egyptian home. Some nice furniture might make it all better. Well, furniture in ancient Egypt was sometimes built into the house. The chairs and tables might be part of the walls!

I am important.

I am VERY important.

Some richer ancient Egyptians did have chairs. The more important you were, the higher your chair. Hopefully you're not a rich kid afraid of heights.

Your oven might take twice as long to cook dinner since it's just made of stone and fire. There were no fridges, either. Ancient Egyptians would dig a pit below ground to keep food cool. Imagine having to dig a hole every time you want a cool drink or snack!

Now, where did I bury that ice lolly?

FISHy Business

Fizzy drinks and fruit juices didn't always exist. Those things had to be made, and some of the ingredients were hard or impossible to get in ancient Egypt. Water, on the other hand, is one drink that has always been around. Fortunately for Egyptians, the Nile was right there on the doorstep!

I think it's time to sell some magic beans for a cow!

Unfortunately, the water in the Nile was not safe to drink. If you were rich, you might be able to grab a cup of milk to <u>quench</u> your thirst, but milk was often too expensive for the poor.

"This is so dry."

Finding something good to eat was just as tricky in ancient Egypt. Poor people could not afford meat, so expect to be eating meals of bread and vegetables. Good luck making a decent sandwich out of those! If milk is off the cards, that means no cheese or butter, either.

So, maybe not all meat was for the rich. Poor people might have been able to get hold of some fish to eat. However, fishing was risky business. Some fish were sacred, so you might find yourself in big trouble if you eat the wrong one!

I'M SACRED! DON'T EAT ME!

NO, HE'S NOT! I AM! Or I could be.

Eaten by THE GODS

Just like the ancient Greeks, Romans and Vikings, the ancient Egyptians worshipped lots of gods and goddesses. However, Egyptian gods were a little bit different. They didn't look quite so... human.

Did they worship aliens? No, but those gods did look strange!

Ancient Egyptian gods weren't from another planet, but they did look quite strange. Many gods of ancient Egypt were often shown as human-like, which mostly meant they walked on two legs. Other than that, they had the heads of beasts and the bodies of... other beasts!

My favourite god is Sobek. He has the head of a crocodile!

If you wanted to ask a god for something, you had to pray to the temple gods. They would pass on your message to the right god. If you didn't get what you wanted, you could visit the temple and give the temple god statue a little whack with a reed to show them that you were not happy. However, don't go doing something like that to the scary ones or bad things might happen!

WHACK!

OUCH!

Call me 'Sobek' one more time and I WILL eat you!

Some of the gods were feared by most people in ancient Egypt. Ammit, who also had a crocodile head, was one. The ancient Egyptians believed that if you did something really bad, Ammit might magically appear in the afterlife and eat you up. She certainly had the teeth to do so!

Horrible HAIRSTYLES

You won't be laughing in a moment...

Do you sometimes worry about getting bad haircuts? Well, the haircuts in ancient Egypt were permanently bad. If you think the adults' haircuts look silly, you're not prepared for the kids'...

For pretty much all of their childhoods, ancient Egyptian children had to wear a haircut called the Lock of Youth. Their entire heads would be shaved apart from one braided lock of hair on the side of their head.

Who came up with this hairstyle?

SPLINTERS and Senet

There was no plastic to make lots of different, interesting toys back in ancient Egypt. There were no electronics, either, meaning no video games. So, what on earth did children play with?

The ancient Egyptians made many toys from materials such as wood. They made dice, gameboards and toy animals. They even made dolls. Be careful you don't get too many splinters!

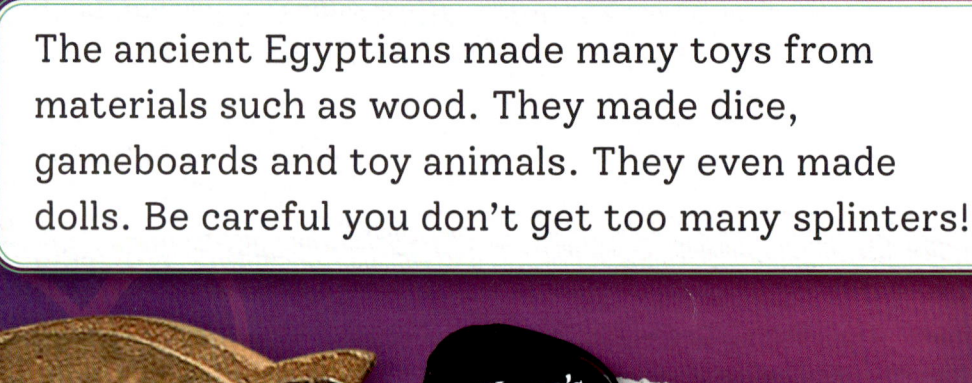

Where's the fun in splinters?

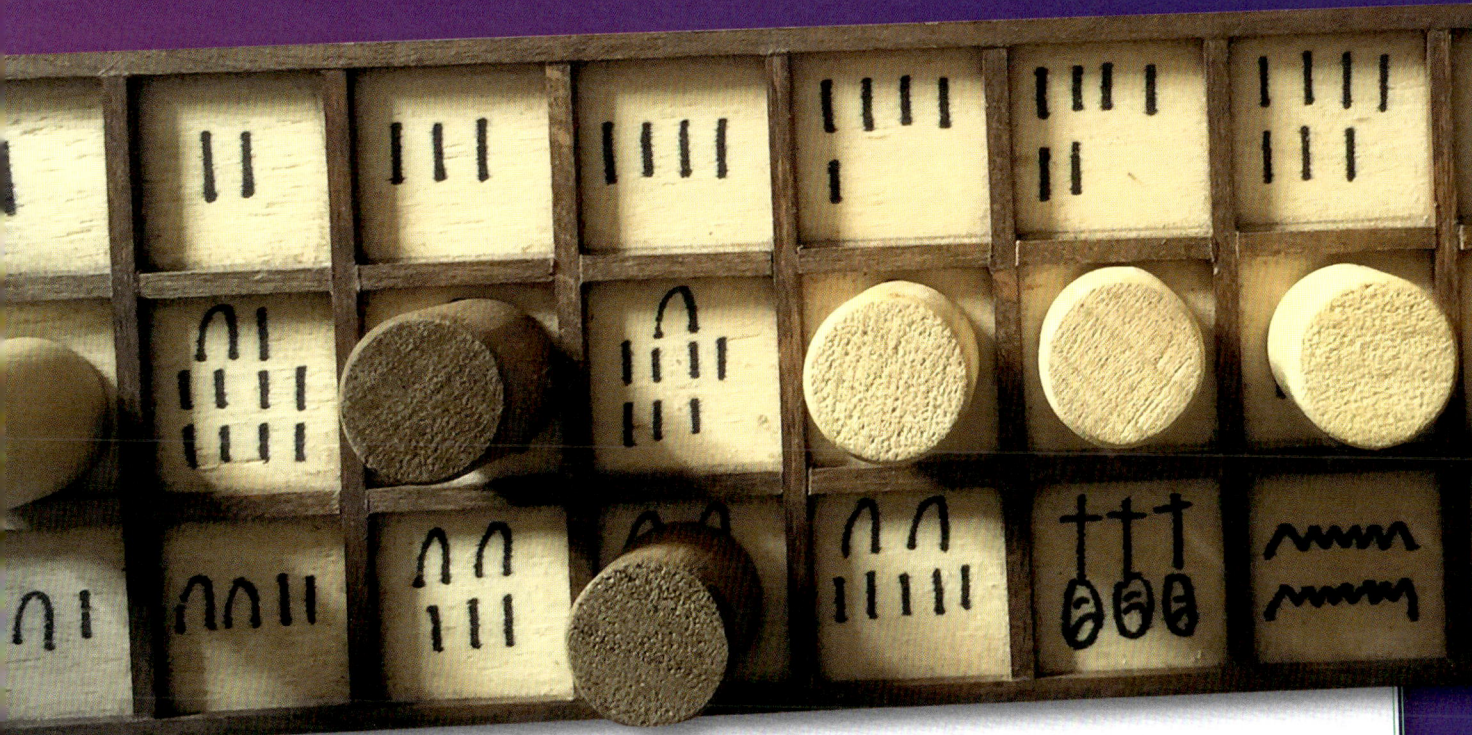

One board game that the ancient Egyptians played was called Senet. The board had 30 squares and each player had five playing pieces. The winner is the first person to get all of their pieces off the board.

To find out how many spaces you could move on the board, you had to throw sticks... or bones! You had better get used to the idea of playing games with bones in ancient Egypt. It was often easier to find bones than a dice!

Gross! I don't want to play anymore!

Writing in PICTURES

Most kids in ancient Egypt did not go to school. Don't cheer yet, though! Many were still expected to learn some of the basics. Yet, the basics in ancient Egypt weren't exactly basic, were they?

Those are some funny looking numbers!

Children usually started school at around age four. They were mostly taught by their parents, so let's hope your parents know their stuff! Children learnt how to work more than anything.

"But I'm trying my hardest!"

Boys would learn the family trade. That means they would be working the same job as their parent, usually their father. They were expected to take over from their dads one day. However, if a boy failed to do the job well, he might even be sent away to set up his life in another town!

Some girls might get to learn to become doctors. For most, this was not the case. Many girls learnt how to look after a home. This included learning how to cook and sew, or even take care of the family business.

"My brother got sent away, so now I have to do his job!"

"Mum gave me this shopping list, but I don't think they have all these animals at the store!"

Many children were taught to read and write as well as do basic mathematics. However, reading and writing was done very differently in ancient Egypt. They wrote most things in hieroglyphics.

Hieroglyphics

Hieroglyphics look like pictures instead of letters. However, they weren't always written from side to side like you might be reading these words. In ancient Egypt, words were often written going down a page.

GROWN UP
at WHAT age?

Adulthood came much earlier in ancient Egypt. Boys became adults at around 14 while girls became adults at around 12. That's quite a few years sooner than kids today. Finally, no more bossy adults telling you what you can and can't do!

I'll never get to do what I want!

However, if your parents weren't telling you what to do, everyone else would. Only rich people really got a say in what they did after growing up. There were plenty of things you might have to do to survive!

Girls might be married at 12 years old. They would leave their families to move in with their husband's family. Their new home would probably be just as crowded as the old one, but without their own family within its walls.

This new family is even bigger!

I don't want a job at 14!

Children would begin working at around age 14, whether they wanted a job or not. Do you have a dream job that you wouldn't mind doing at 14? Well, let's hope your dream is to follow in your parent's footsteps. All that training wasn't for nothing, you know!

There were some strange and difficult jobs in ancient Egypt that you would be wishing you didn't have to do. Hopefully one of them isn't your parent's job!

I wish my dad had a better job.

A scribe was someone who wrote things down. That sounds simple enough! It could even help you move up in the world. However, I hope you have lots of time on your hands. Remember, scribes would have to write in hieroglyphics!

Which letter is 'A' again? The bird or the lion?

I came here to catch fish, not wrestle crocodiles!

Fishermen often worked around the Nile, which could be dangerous. First, you need to make sure you aren't catching any sacred fish. Next, you've got to deal with the crocodiles!

For some ancient Egyptians, their jobs meant getting even closer to the Nile. Laundry was often washed by the riverbank. If you were able to escape the crocodiles, you might still be covered in filth!

That crocodile stole my socks!

That's TOUGH!

Are you still thinking that being a kid today is tough? What a relief that it's nowhere near as tough as ancient Egypt! From crocodile gods to terrible haircuts, ancient Egypt was not a fun time to be a kid... and that's if you survived your childhood.

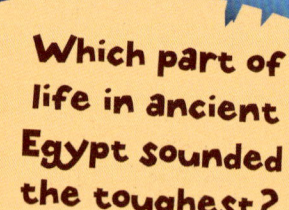

Which part of life in ancient Egypt sounded the toughest?

You can forget your worries, though. Relax back into the present. You don't need to write all day in hieroglyphics and no one will give you a Lock of Youth haircut... probably. Now, let's get back to enjoying being a kid here and now.

GLOSSARY

afterlife	the life that some people believe people will have after their bodies have died
amulets	a charm that is worn to keep away bad spirits
anklets	jewellery worn around the ankle
armlets	jewellery worn around the upper arm
BC	meaning 'before Christ', it is used to mark dates that occurred before the starting year of most calendars
diseases	illnesses that affect a person
electronics	anything that runs off electricity
ingredients	things that are used to make something
medicine	to do with healing and helping the body
natural	something not made or caused by people
quench	to satisfy a thirst
reeds	tall, thin woody plants
sacred	highly important in religion
symbols	something that stands in for another thing
temple	a place where a god or gods are worshipped
valley	a long stretch of land between mountains or hills
worshipped	love being shown to something important such as a god
woven	made by crossing threads or other long pieces of material over and under each other

INDEX

amulets 19

anklets 19

armlets 19

chairs 13

crocodiles 16–17, 29–30

doctors 8–9, 23

families 4, 10, 12, 23, 27

fishing 15, 29

gods 16–17, 30

hieroglyphics 24, 28, 30

jewellery 19

jobs 23, 27–29

Lock of Youth 18, 30

Nile, the 6, 14, 29

papyrus 7, 12, 25

reeds 12, 17, 25

temples 17

Photo Credits All images are courtesy of Shutterstock.com, unless otherwise specified. With thanks to Getty Images, Thinkstock Photo and iStockphoto.

Recurring images - YamabikaY, Tartila, TADDEUS, sumkinn, Vlada Young, Gaidamashchuk, pics five, Andrey_Kuzmin, Macrovector, Jemastock, Milano M, Oligo22, ONYXprj. Cover - Fedor Selivanov, Marti Bug Catcher, Kabardins photo. 2-3 - Gordana Adzieva. 4-5 - donatas1205, AlexAnton, New Africa, rangizzz, VaLiza. 6-7 - Alfmaler, Krakenimages.com, Lapina, Marco Ossino, Merydolla, Mind Pixell. 8-9 - 4 PM production, Everilda, Olga Kuevda, robuart, RHJPhtotos, SIRNARM USAVICH. 10-11 - BearFotos, Dmytro Buianskyi, Jaroslav Moravcik. 12-13 - Dunhill, Ievgenii Meyer, MasaMima, matryoshka, Matyas Rehak, Phakorn Kasikij, Quintanilla. 14-15 - bildfokus.se, Litvalifa, Monkey Business Images, SpicyTruffel, tan_tan, Victoria Sergeeva. 16-17 - Evil Panda (Wikimedia Commons), Hogan Imaging, matryoshka, Nomad_Soul, Paul Vinten, Valadzionak Volha. 18-19 - Captmondo (WikimediaCommons), grmarc, Macrovector, NotionPic, Olena Brodetska, Radiokafka. 20-21 - Beatrice Barberis, Creativa Images, Einsamer Schütze (Wikimedia Commons), Kateryna Onyshchuk, Oscar Peralta Anechina, Perfect_kebab. 22-23 - BNP Design Studio, Body Stock, matryoshka, GoodStudio, Red Fox studio. 24-25 - amelipulen, Anastasiia Kulikovska, Mega Pixel, Photick. 26-27 - amelipulen, ESB Professional, matryoshka, pink.mousy, Prostock-studio. 28-29 - GolF2532, gualtiero boffi, Laboo Studio, nattanan726, NotionPic, OlegDoroshin, Olga Kuevda. 30 - VaLiza.